Little Bug

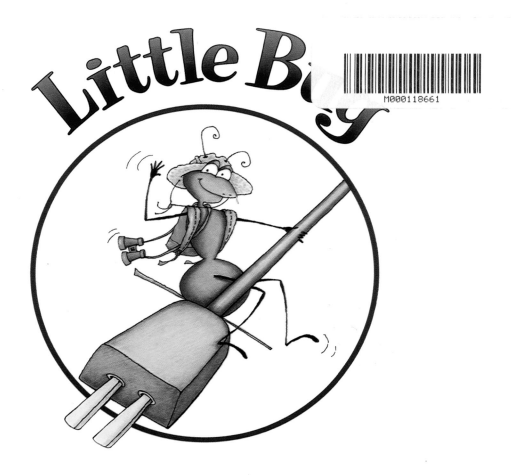

Written by Jacklyn Williams and Linda Clark-Ford
Illustrated by Liisa Chauncy Guida

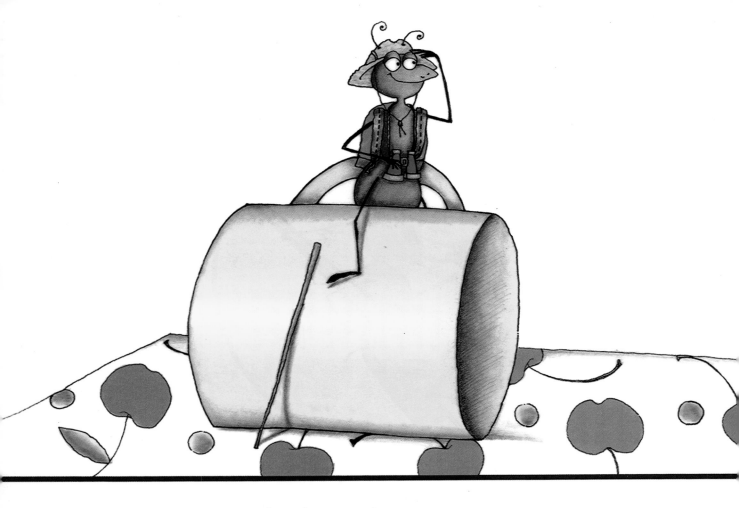

Little bug is on a mug.

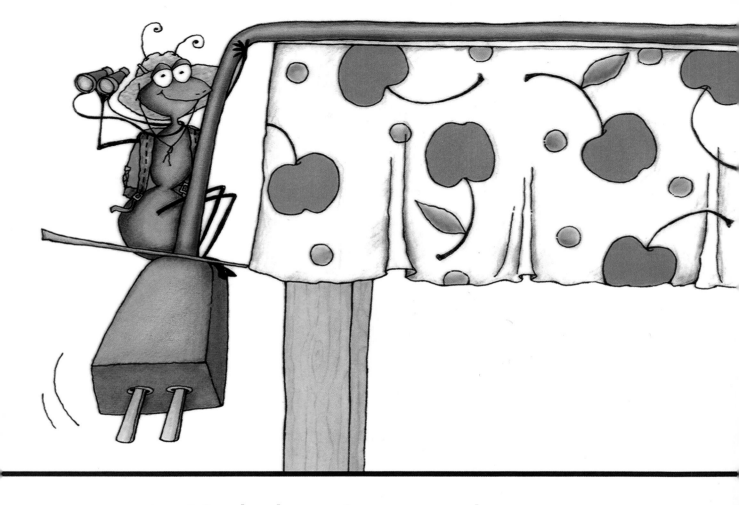

Little bug is on a plug.

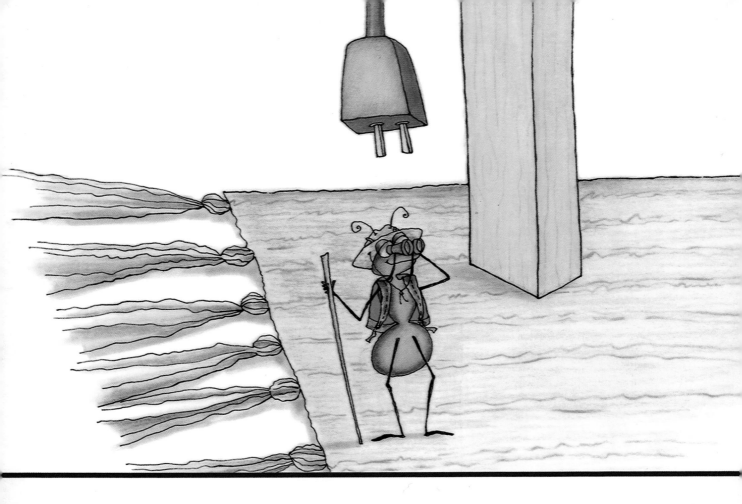

Little bug is on a rug.

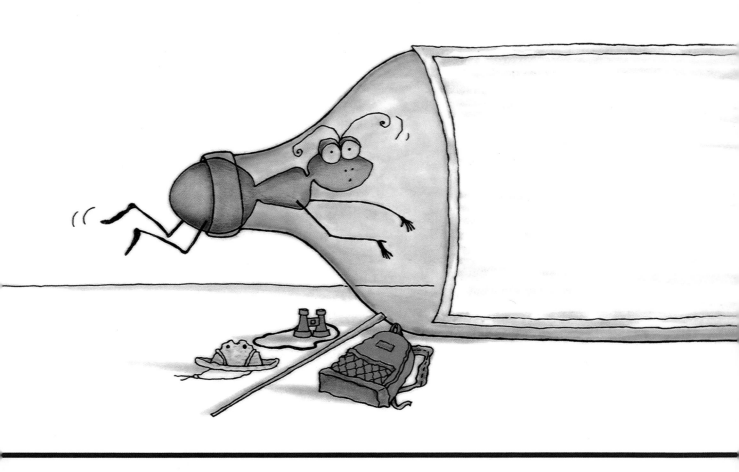

Little bug is in a jug.

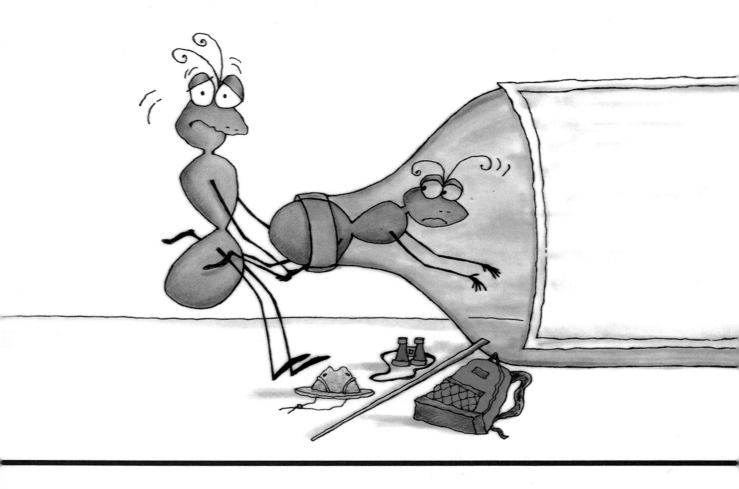

Tug!

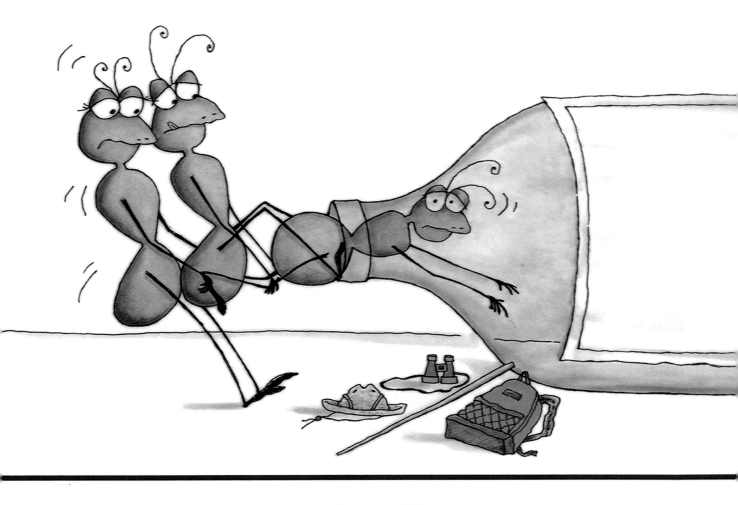

Tug! Tug! Tug!

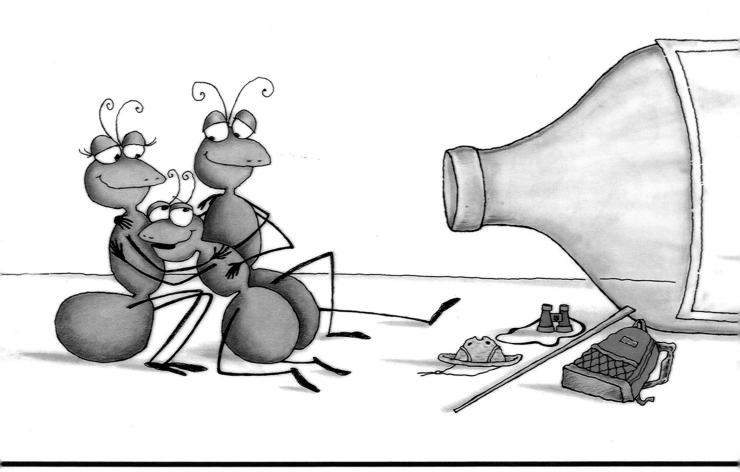

Hug! Hug! Hug!